Name:

....

School:

....

Class:

....

On this page, the ‹y› at the end of each word makes an /ee/ sound.

jolly   daisy   muddy   teddy

sunny   funny   daddy   spotty

Read the words in the logs. Match each word to the right picture.

sunny

body

puppy

teddy

sandy

holly

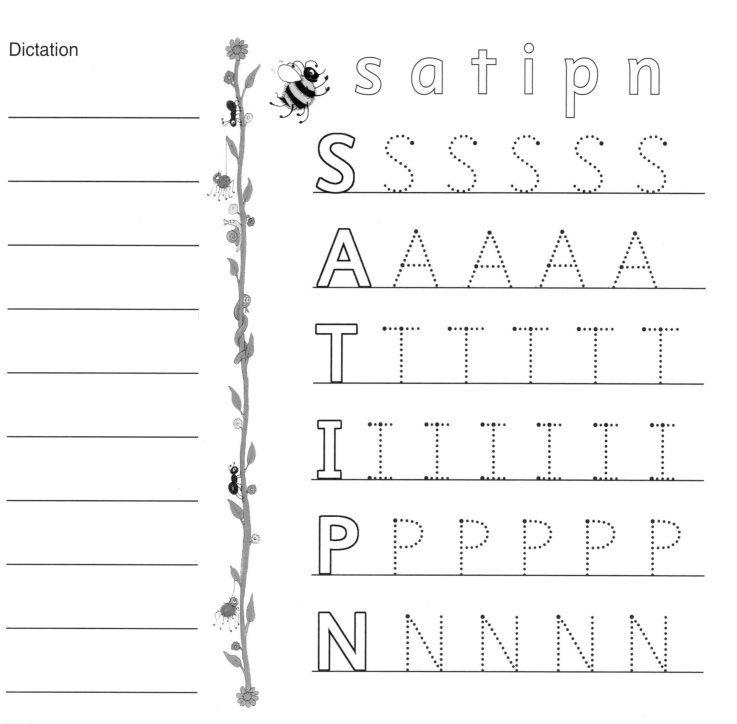

s a t i p n

S S S S S S

A A A A A A

T T T T T T

I I I I I I

P P P P P P

N N N N N N

Write inside the outline letters and match the capital letters to the lower-case letters.

Tricky words

you

your

Look Say the letters.	Copy then Cover	Write then Check	Have another go!
you	you		
your	your		

Write inside the vowel letters using a blue pen or pencil.
Then find the vowels in the grid and color the squares with a short vowel in blue.

a

e

i

o

u

s	m	d	e	n	i	t	c
h	a	r	l	u	j	p	x
o	z	t	i	g	a	b	y
t	e	k	h	o	z	m	e
q	n	a	f	u	s	l	g
p	o	z	k	m	i	h	u

the hen

Choose one of the short vowel sounds, /a/, /e/, /i/, /o/, or /u/, to make the words.

f u n	h _ p	r _ d	b _ g
m _ n	p _ t	c _ p	m _ p
s _ ck	sh _ p	cl _ p	qu _ ck

bag   a

net   e

bin   i

box   o

mug   u

Ring the short vowel and write the word. Color the pictures.

a e i (o) u

b o x

a e i o u

a e i o u

a e i o u

a e i o u

a e i o u

a e i o u

a e i o u

a e i o u

Dictation

_____

_____

_____

_____

_____

_____

_____

_____

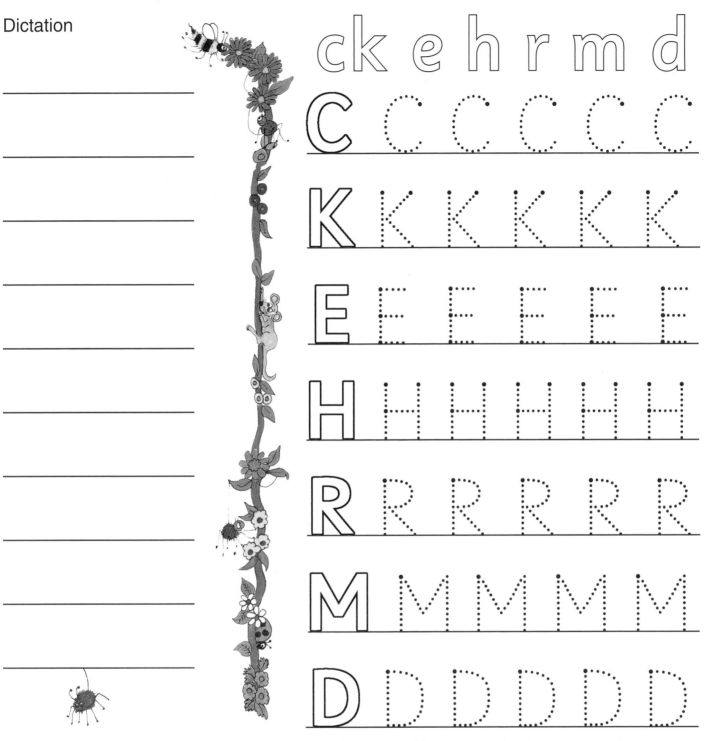

c k e h r m d

C C C C C C C

K K K K K K K

E E E E E E E

H H H H H H H

R R R R R R R

M M M M M M M

D D D D D D D

Write inside the outline letters and match the capital letters to the lower-case letters.

R   e   d   E   K   M

C   c   r   D   h   k   m   H

come

Tricky words

some

Read the words in the flowers below and join the pairs.
Find the flowers containing the words "some" and "come" and color these flowers yellow.

Look Say the letters.	Copy then Cover	Write then Check	Have another go!
come	come		
some	some		

8

in the
park

_____

_____

_____

_____

_____

_____

Join each word to the right picture.

swing   dog   picnic   tree

In words containing a short vowel sound, the /ck/ sound is written with a ‹c› and a ‹k›.

duck   bricks   sack   peck   black

sock   jacket   tick   kick   clock

Write over the dotted words and draw a picture for each word in the rockets.

Dictation

_____

_____

_____

_____

_____

_____

_____

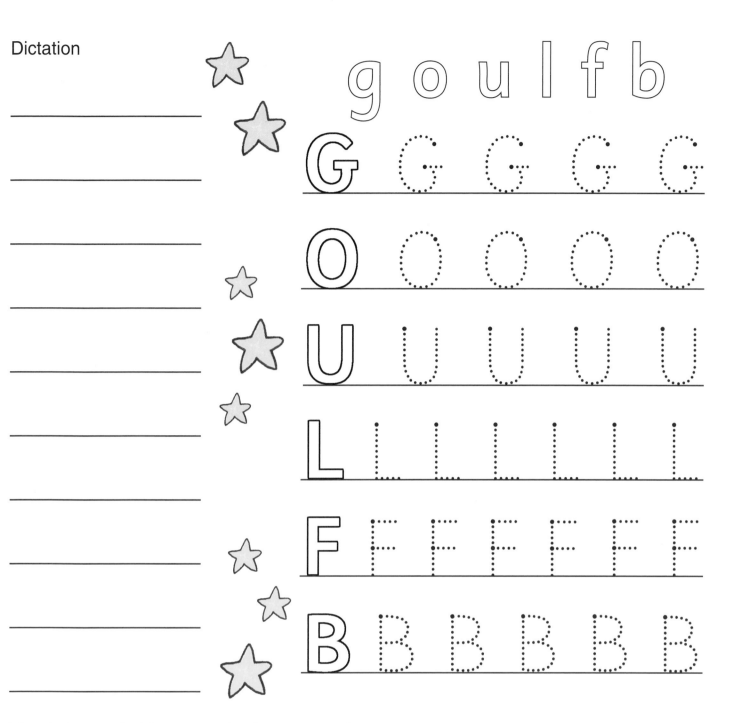

g o u l f b

G G G G G

O O O O O

U U U U U

L L L L L L L L

F F F F F F

B B B B B B

Match the capital letters to the lower-case letters.

Read each phrase and draw a picture in the frame to illustrate it.

a spotty dog

a fluffy cat

a green frog

an oak tree

a big clock

a running man

Tricky words

said

here

there

Look Say the letters.	**Copy** then **Cover**	**Write** then **Check**	**Have another go!**
said	said		
here	here		
there	there		

Write the word underneath each picture. Color the pictures.

bed

_ _ _

_ _ _

_ _ _

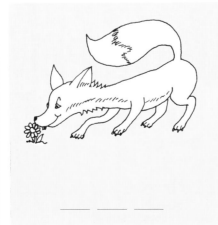
_ _ _

_ _ _

the pond

_____

_____

_____

_____

Join each word to the right picture.

rocks   duckling

toad

boat

When two letters that make the same sound are next to each other, the sound is only said once.

parrot   egg   bell   jazz   button

kitten   huff   bill   doll   miss

Read the word and draw a picture to go with it.

rabbit

dress

duck

shell

puppet

carrot

Dictation

Write inside the capital letters and join them to the matching lower-case letters.

_____

_____

_____

_____

_____

_____

_____

_____

T L D C

G g t l d J

H h u c U

P p a m A

F b n j M

K f i E

e k r

B I R N

Trace inside the letter sounds below and write over the dotted letters.

j J J J J J J J J

ai oa ie ee or

16

Tricky words

they

Look Say the letters.	**Copy** then **Cover**	**Write** then **Check**	**Have another go!**
they	they		

Choose the right word and write it underneath the picture.

met mat man

mat

log dig dog

____

cup cut cap

____

peg egg leg

____

net nut not

____

and ant act

____

three trick tree

____

boot book boat

____

jar jet jam

____

17

the fox

_____

_____

_____

_____

_____

Join each word to the right picture.

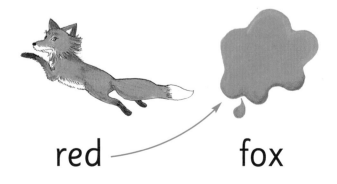 

red   fox   nest   bat

In words with a "hop-over e" digraph, the ‹e› at the end does not say /e/; it uses its magic to hop back over the consonant and turns the short vowel into a long vowel sound.

smoke use game eve mule

hive these joke shave side

Join each leaf to the right tree.

Pete

bone

cake

smile

nose

cube

smile

skate

rope

kite

Dictation

Write inside each outline letter and then write the matching capital or lower-case letter in the space next to it.

_____

_____

_____

_____

_____

_____

_____

_____

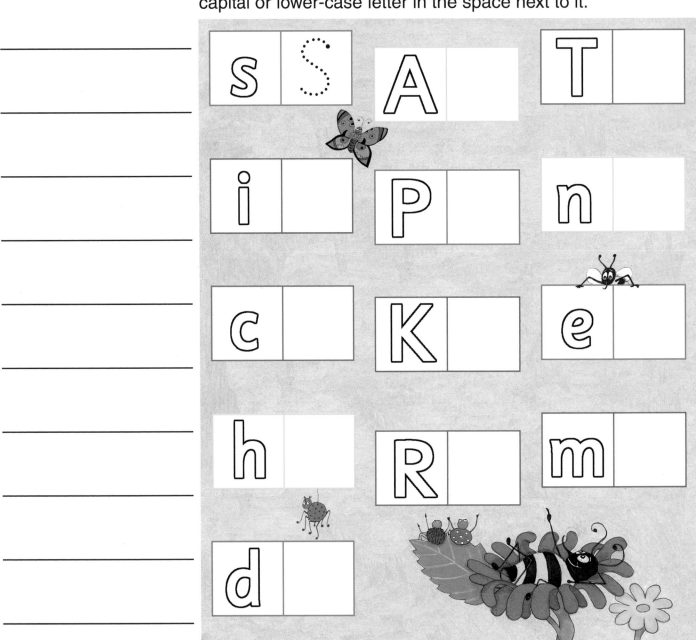

Write inside the outline letters and then write over the dotted capital letters.

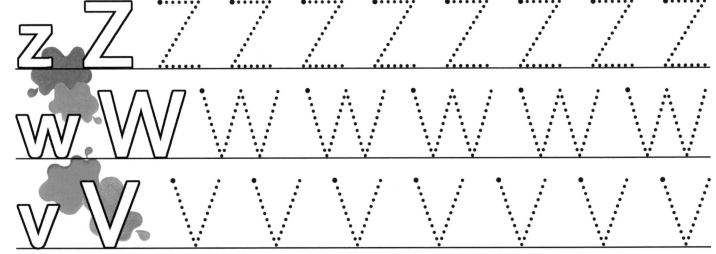

Tricky words

go **no** **so**

Read the words and then find them in the wordsearch.

no **your** **go** **here** **they**

a	c	o	m	e	b	s	o
s	a	i	d	d	t	p	f
n	o	p	a	y	o	u	m
h	e	r	e	c	d	x	z
q	u	m	t	h	e	r	e
y	o	u	r	f	h	g	o
k	s	j	x	t	h	e	y
c	z	s	o	m	e	r	w

said **so**

there **some**

you **come**

Look Say the letters.	Copy then Cover	Write then Check	Have another go!
go	go		
no	no		
so	so		

21

the fish

_____

_____

_____

_____

Match each word to the right sea creature.

catfish   starfish   flatfish   eel

Dictation

_____

_____

_____

_____

_____

_____

_____

_____

_____

Write the capital or lower-case letter in the space next to its matching letter.

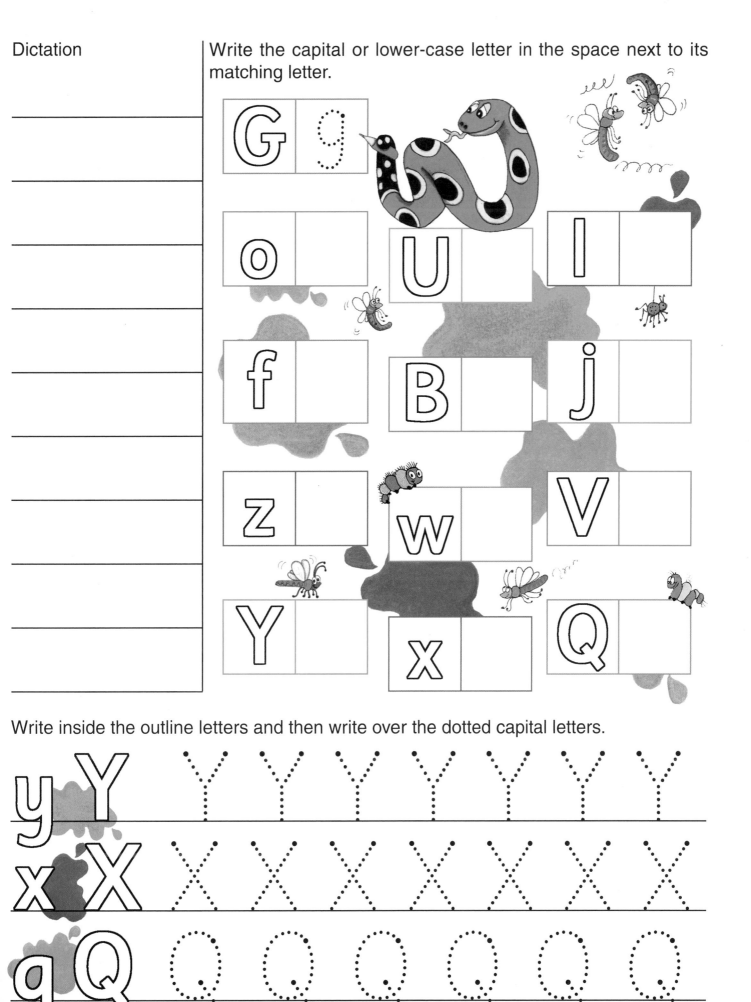

Write inside the outline letters and then write over the dotted capital letters.

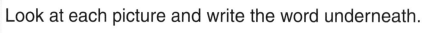

Look at each picture and write the word underneath.

Tricky words

c u e

_____

_____

my

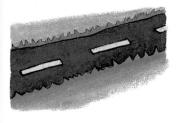

_____

one

3

by

_____

Look Say the letters.	Copy then Cover	Write then Check	Have another go!
my	my		
one	one		
by	by		

24

night time

Join each word to the right picture.

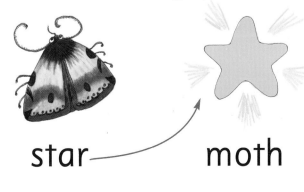

star   moth

sleeping

moon

Choose the right spelling of the /ai/ sound for each picture.

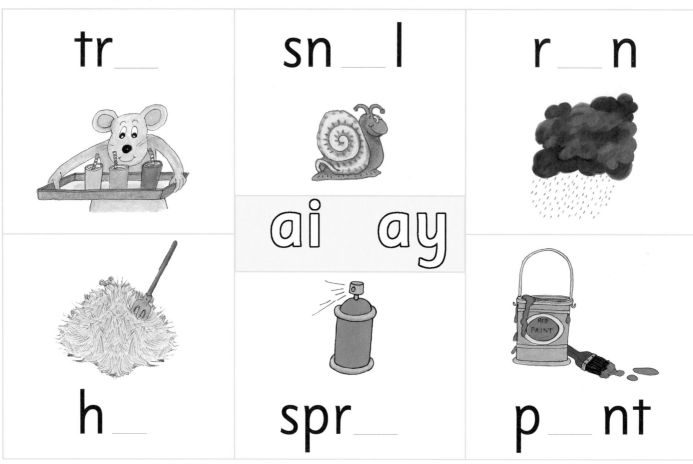

tr___

sn__l

r__n

ai ay

h__

spr___

p__nt

Choose the right spelling of the /oi/ sound for each picture.

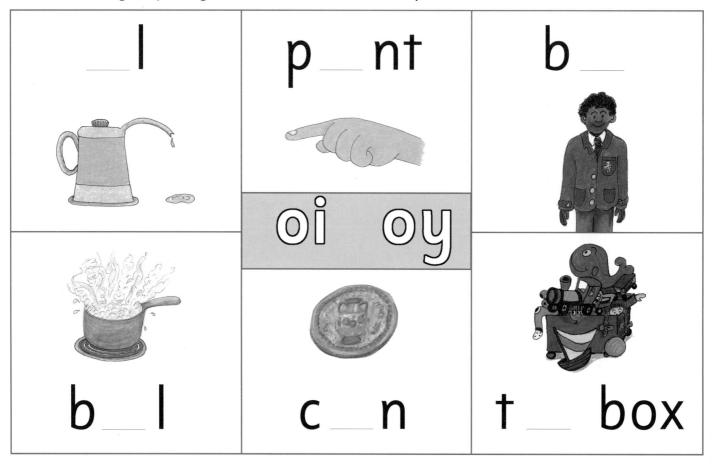

__l

p__nt

b__

oi oy

b__l

c__n

t__ box

Dictation

Write the sections of the alphabet in red, yellow, green and blue.

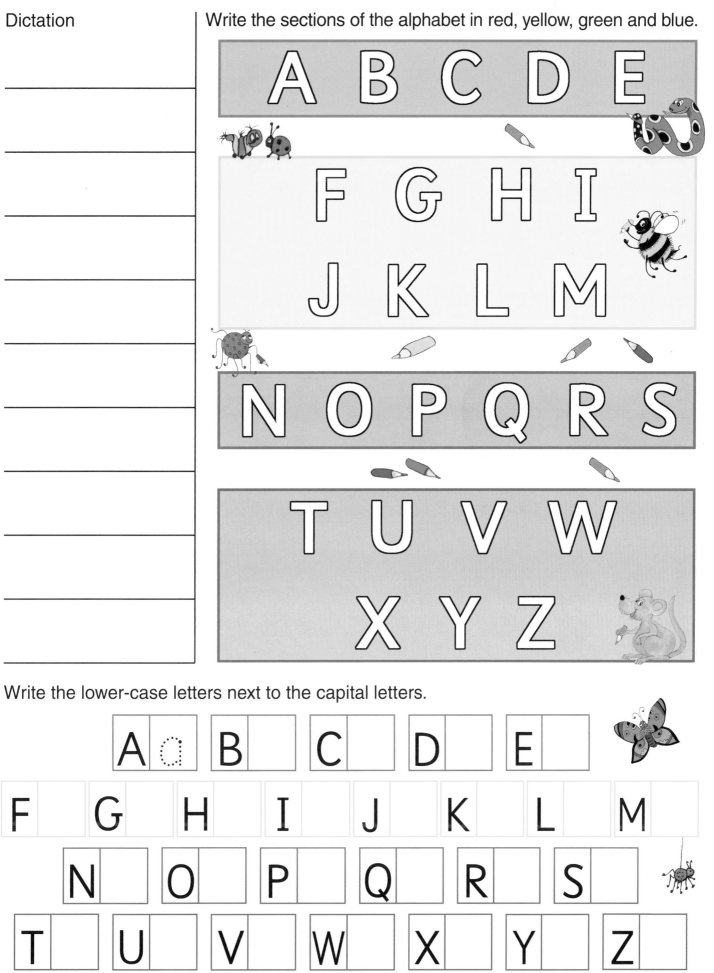

A B C D E

F G H I
J K L M

N O P Q R S

T U V W
X Y Z

Write the lower-case letters next to the capital letters.

A a   B   C   D   E

F   G   H   I   J   K   L   M

N   O   P   Q   R   S

T   U   V   W   X   Y   Z

27

Tricky words

Look Say the letters.	Copy then Cover	Write then Check	Have another go!
only	only		
old	old		

Animal anagrams: put the letters in the right order.

	n t a		n s a i l		g t o a
	e e p s h		k a r s h		r b a c o f x
	k a y		i c h c k		o f x

28

ducks

_____

_____

_____

_____

_____

Animal anagrams: put the letters in the right order.

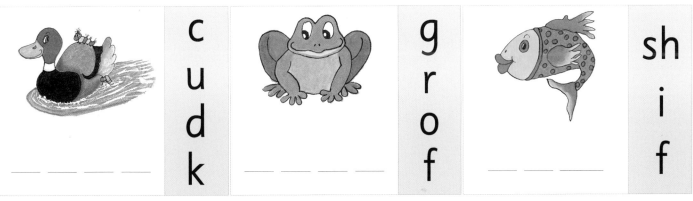

c u d k

g r o f

sh i f

29

The /ee/ sound can be written ‹ee› or ‹ea›.

Read the words at the top of the page and write the correct word under each picture.

ee

three   teeth   tree

leaf   feet   sheep

seal   bee   sea

ea

sheep

_____

_____

_____

_____

_____

_____

_____

_____

Dictation

Write the capital letter next to the lower-case letter.

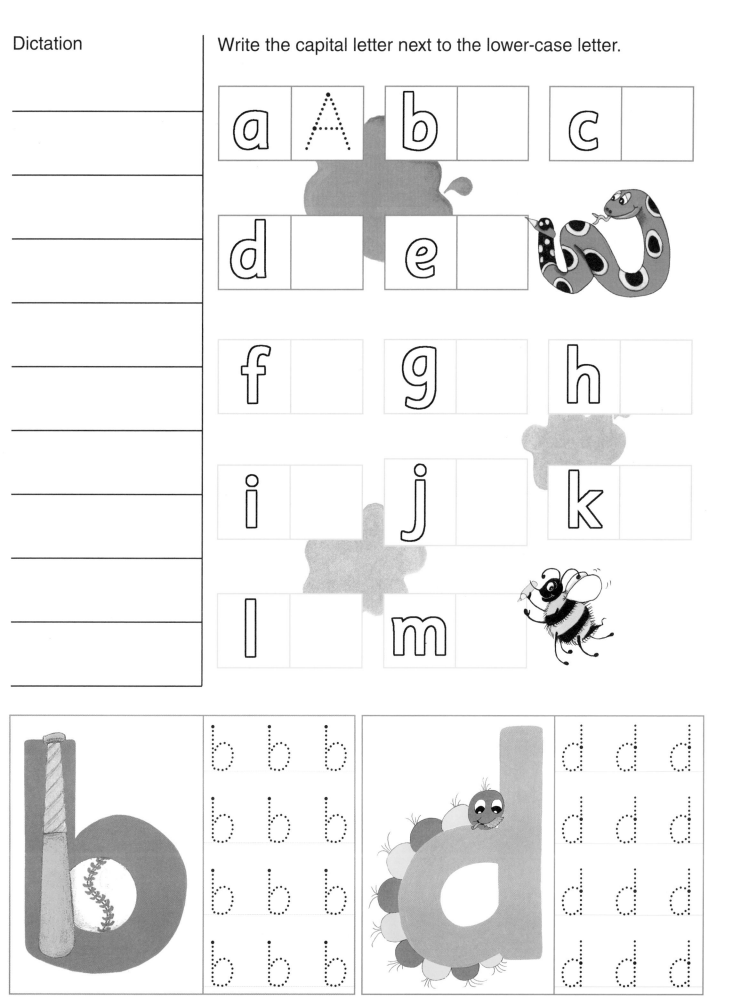

31

Tricky words

like

have

Look at the pictures and choose a /b/ or /d/ sound.

b e d   _og   _at

cra_   pon_   _ook

win__y   te___y   ra__it

Look Say the letters.	Copy then Cover	Write then Check	Have another go!
like	like		
have	have		

32

the
queen

Practice writing ‹b› and ‹d›.

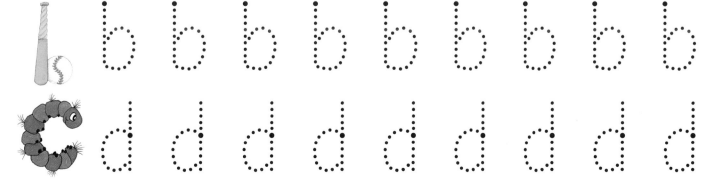

b b b b b b b b b

d d d d d d d d d

pie   lie   line   time   my   flying

tried   cries   sunshine   shy   sky

tie   die   drive   slide   drying   try

Read the words in the stars and draw pictures in the moons to illustrate each word.

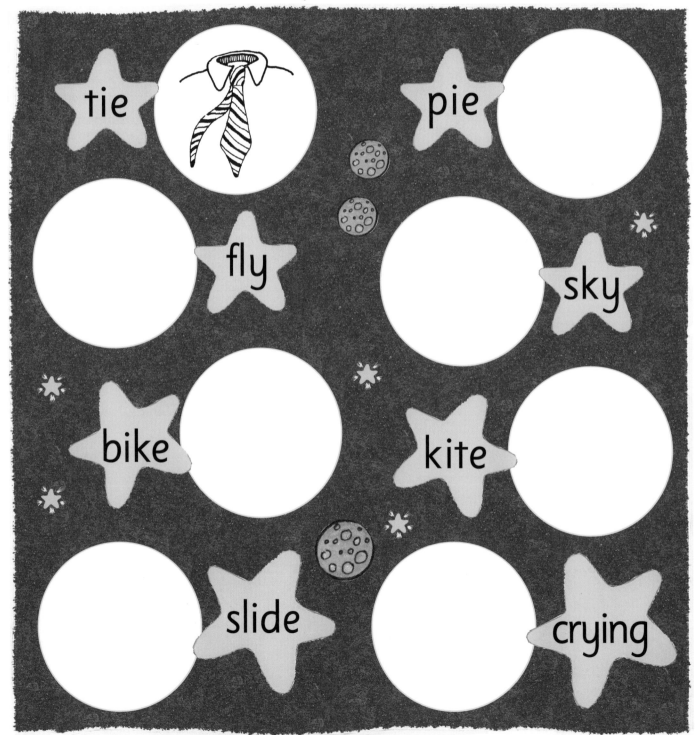

34

Dictation

Write the capital letter next to the lower-case letter.

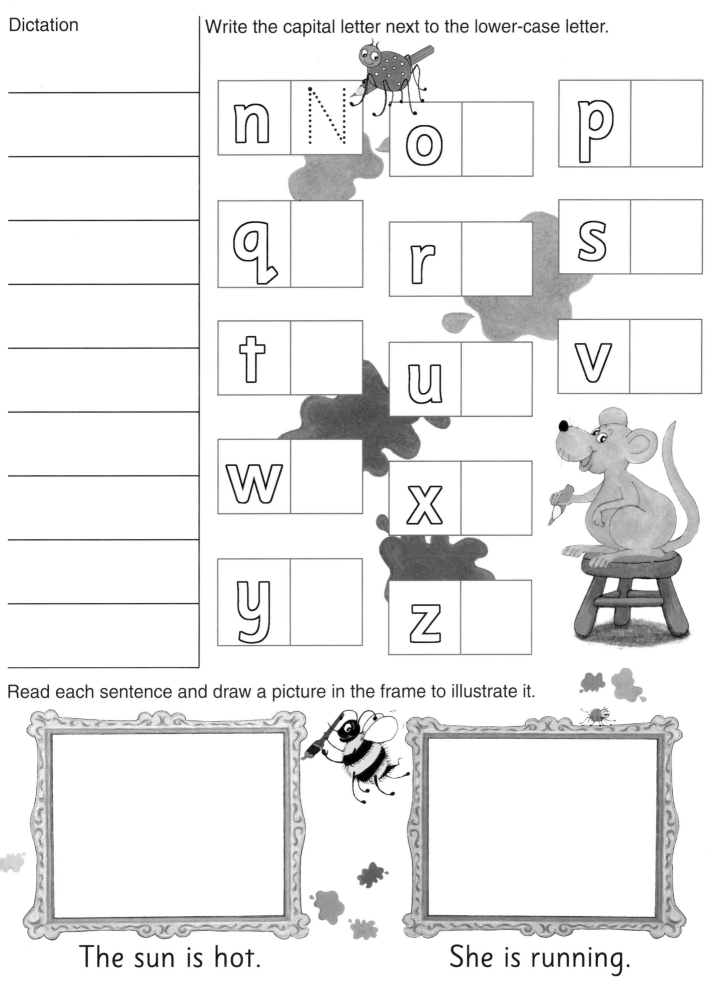

n | N
o |
p |
q |
r |
s |
t |
u |
v |
w |
x |
y |
z |

Read each sentence and draw a picture in the frame to illustrate it.

The sun is hot.

She is running.

Tricky words

live   give

have   like   live   give

Look Say the letters.	Copy then Cover	Write then Check	Have another go!
live	live		
give	give		

Choose the right word and write it underneath the picture.

cub   cube

_____

fin   fine

_____

hug   huge

_____

tub   tube

_____

hat   hate

_____

rid   ride

_____

digging
for
treasure

Write over these "caterpillar c" shapes.

On this page, the ‹ow› digraph says /ou/ and /oa/.

shout south
mouse flour

town brown
owl   flower

Read each word inside the clouds and boats and draw a picture to illustrate it.

cloud

crown

owl

boat

arrow

snow

coat   toad
oak   soap

grow borrow
yellow slow

Dictation

_____

_____

_____

_____

_____

_____

_____

_____

Practice writing these "caterpillar c" letters.

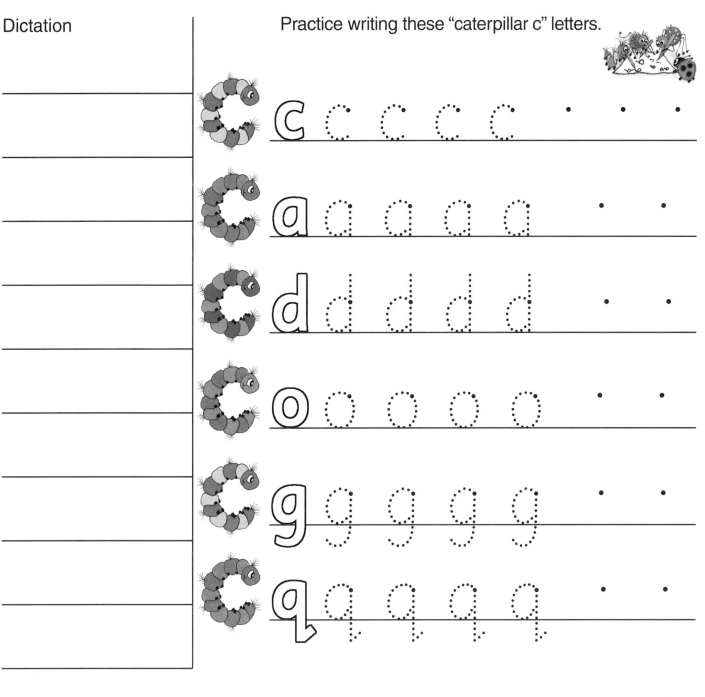

Look at each picture and write the word underneath. Color the pictures.

_____   _____   _____

little

Tricky words

down

Read the words and then find them in the wordsearch.

my   give   one   have   old   little   like   only   by   live   down

l	i	k	e	n	b	m	y
d	f	g	h	a	v	e	f
d	o	w	n	l	i	v	e
o	n	e	s	c	b	y	z
g	u	m	t	s	e	r	u
o	l	d	r	o	n	l	y
k	s	g	i	v	e	r	p
j	p	l	i	t	t	l	e

Look Say the letters.	Copy then Cover	Write then Check	Have another go!
little	little		
down	down		

40

the
shipwreck

_____

_____

_____

_____

_____

Match each word to the right sea creature.

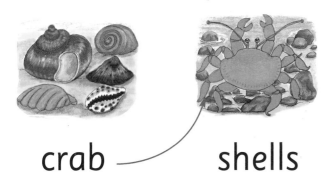 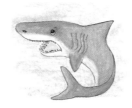 

crab   shells   lobster   shark

The /er/ sound can be written ‹er›, ‹ir›, or ‹ur›.

Read each word and draw a picture inside the shape.

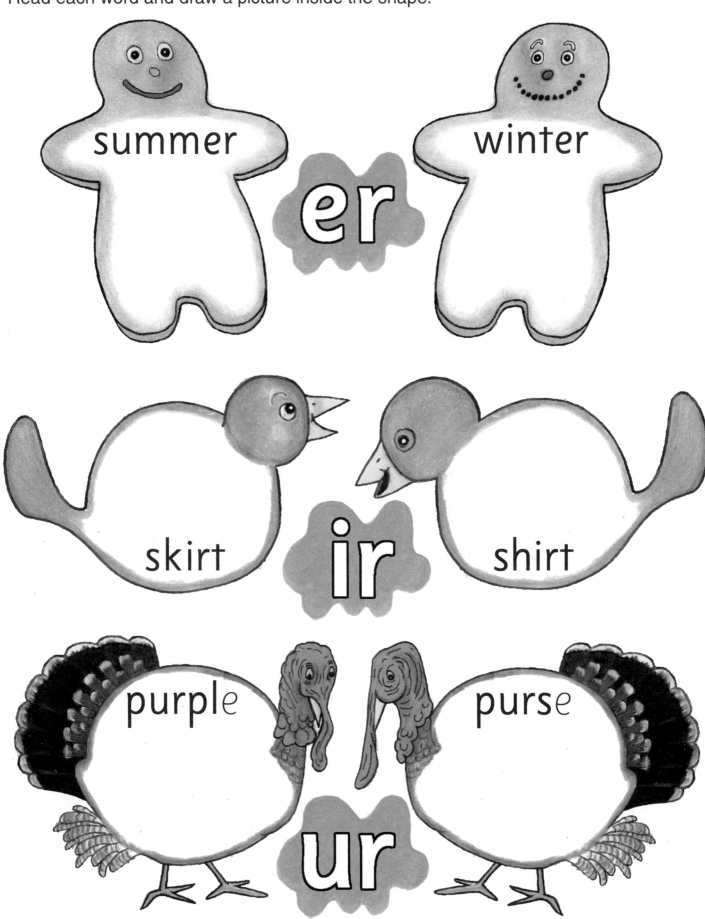

summer

winter

er

skirt

shirt

ir

purple

purse

ur

Dictation

Practice writing the tall letters.

_____

_____

_____

_____

_____

_____

_____

_____

b b b b

d d d d

h h h h

k k k k

l l l l l l

t t t t t

Fill in the spaces and color in the letters.

C   E

G   I   J   M

N   P   S

U   W   Y

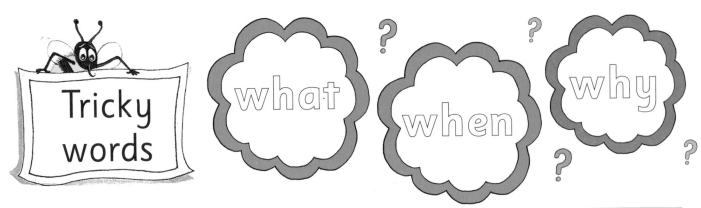

Tricky words

what ? when ? why ?

Look Say the letters.	Copy then Cover	Write then Check	Have another go!
what	what		
when	when		
why	why		

Join each word to the right picture and then color in the pictures.

lie

tree

nail

leek

snail

soap

road

pie

helping
to fix
the car

_____

_____

_____

_____

_____

_____

Join each word to the right vehicle.

bus   jeep   van   car

Dictation

_____

_____

_____

_____

_____

_____

_____

_____

_____

Practice writing these long letters.

g g g g

j j j j j

p p p p

q q q q

y y y y

Can you write the alphabet?

A

46

where

Tricky words

who   which

Look Say the letters.	Copy then Cover	Write then Check	Have another go!
where	where		
who	who		
which	which		

Read each sentence and draw a picture in the frame to illustrate it.

I see the moon and stars.

A boy is asleep in bed.

A duck is swimming on the pond.

The girl has a green dress.

47

the
statue

Join each word to the right picture.

tie   lamb   bird   boot